Reasons My Kid Is Crying*

* We gave him delicious pudding.

GREG PEMBROKE

Creator of reasonsmysoniscrying.tumblr.com

REA·SONS MY KID IS CRY·ING

GREG PEMBROKE

REA·SONS MY KID IS CRY·ING

 THREE RIVERS PRESS · NEW YORK

Published in the United States by Three Rivers Press, an imprint of the Crown
Publishing Group, a division of Random House LLC, a Penguin Random House
Company, New York.
www.crownpublishing.com

Three Rivers Press and the Tugboat design are registered trademarks of
Random House LLC.

Library of Congress Cataloging-in-Publication Data is available upon request.

ISBN 978-0-8041-3983-0
eBook ISBN 978-0-8041-3984-7

Printed in the United States of America

BOOK DESIGN BY ELINA D. NUDELMAN
COVER DESIGN BY JESS MORPHEW
COVER PHOTOGRAPHS: (FRONT) THE PEMBROKE FAMILY; (BACK) CLOCKWISE,
STARTING FROM TOP LEFT: BLAKE; J.S.K.; KATE HALVORSON; MELVIN, CAREY, AND
CADEN LITTON; JESSICA METZGER AND INGRID; THE PEMBROKE FAMILY; ANDREA K.;
THE CHANCE FAMILY

10 9 8 7 6 5 4 3 2 1

First Edition

TO MY FAMILY.
WE LAUGH TOGETHER. WE CRY TOGETHER.
WE MADE A BOOK TOGETHER
(WHILE LAUGHING ABOUT CRYING).

CONTENTS

INTRODUCTION   *11*

PART ONE

1. Great Expectations   *15*

2. Recipe for Disaster   *33*

3. No Shirt, No Shoes, No Tantrum   *53*

4. E.T. . . . The Exasperated Toddler   *69*

5. If You Can't Do the Time   *81*

6. Lost in Translation   *95*

7. Pull-ups and Let-downs   *107*

PART TWO

8. We Are Family   *123*

9. Sibling Rivalry   *137*

PART THREE

10. Call of the Wild   *153*

11. Higher Learning   *169*

12. It's My Party   *185*

ACKNOWLEDGMENTS   *197*

PHOTO CREDITS   *199*

REA·SONS MY KID IS CRY·ING

I BROKE THIS
CHEESE IN HALF.

10

INTRODUCTION

When I decided to change jobs and stay at home two days per week with two sons under two years old, I knew things would get crazy, but no one could have predicted how crazy they would get. Kids cry for any and all reasons—and despite how hard you try to prevent the meltdowns, they still crash down on your head like so many waves of tortured sadness. Desperate to find a laugh in this sea of tears, I started snapping pictures midtantrum. Nearly two years into this experiment in Daddy Daycare, my Tumblr blog *Reasons My Son Is Crying* was born. Part documentary, part therapy, and completely hilarious, submissions immediately began pouring in from parents around the world. This collection of photos—from both my house and families across six continents—is a glimpse into the tribulations of parenthood and a sweet reminder to find a way to laugh at these tumultuous, tedious, and terrible twos. And threes. And fours. Maybe fives.

PART ONE

HE'S NOT ALLOWED
TO PICK UP
DOG POOP.

14

1

GREAT EXPECTATIONS

Like tiny Bond villains with very small and insanely specific goals, toddlers have great expectations for what life will bring on any given day. Disappoint them at your peril.

HE COULDN'T TAKE
THE GUMDROP
PASS.

IT WASN'T
RAINING
INSIDE.

HE CLIMBED INTO THE DISHWASHER.

I WOULDN'T LET
HIM CRAWL INTO
A 400°F OVEN.

I SAID THE SPONGE IS NOT FOOD.

20

HE CAN'T EAT HIS
DAD'S PHONE.

WE WOULDN'T LET HIM DRAG HIS NEW BOOKSHELF INTO THE LIVING ROOM.

SHE WANTED TO TEAR UP
MY TWENTY-DOLLAR BILL.

I ASKED HER TO PLEASE STOP
LICKING THE BOTTOM OF HER SHOE.

SHE DIDN'T
WANT TO BE A
PRINCESS.

25

DISPATCHES • FROM • THE • FRONT • LINES

The great thing about kids is that because they know so little of the world, everything is new and exciting to them. Recently my son and I were having a great time wrestling on the floor, laughing and giggling—a perfect father-son moment.

That is, until he started staring at my hands. I guess he had never noticed my knuckles before. He hated the look of that weird, wrinkly, bunched-up skin—and started tugging on it, demanding that I "take it off." When I explained that it just wasn't possible for me to rip off my own knuckles, our fun-filled afternoon wrestlefest turned into the eighth sobbing fit of the day.

WE TOLD HIM THAT HE WAS TOO YOUNG FOR BEER.

SWIMMING IN THE DOG'S WATER BOWL WASN'T AS FUN AS SHE THOUGHT IT WOULD BE.

HE GOT STUCK.

THE NEIGHBOR'S DOG
ISN'T OUTSIDE.

THE DOG WOULD
NOT SIT STILL LONG
ENOUGH FOR HIM
TO EAT HER TAIL.

just lik

HE ATE HIS PEACH,
THEN GOT MAD THAT
HIS PEACH WAS GONE.

2
RECIPE FOR DISASTER

Parents know that nutritious, homemade meals are necessary to make sure that your kids grow up healthy and strong. Toddlers know that mealtime is a broccoli-filled Thunderdome where only the strongest, smartest, and fastest will survive.

I MADE HIM CHICKEN NUGGETS—AKA HIS FAVORITE MEAL.

HIS INSTANT
OATMEAL WAS
NOT, IN FACT,
INSTANT.

SHE DEMANDED A NEW FORK. NOW SHE WANTS THE OLD FORK BACK.

I WOULDN'T PUT SALT ON HER APRICOTS.

37

HER POPSICLE
WAS COLD.

38

I LET HIM DRINK HIS SMOOTHIE IN THE CAR.

39

THIS TEDDY GRAHAM
LOST ITS HEAD.

40

WE THOUGHT HE
MIGHT LIKE TO
TRY PEAS.

I TOOK THE GLASS OF RED WINE AWAY FROM HER.

WE HAD TO PUT
THE CUPCAKES
INTO THE OVEN
TO BAKE.

43

THE LAST PIECE OF BANANA
FELL OUT OF THE PEEL.

44

THE BANANA IS
OVER.

45

HE WANTED ME TO
PUT THE CRUST BACK
ONTO THE TOAST.

GRANDMA gives
the best HUGS!

I TOLD HER THAT I HAD TO WASH HER FACE AFTER DINNER.

A FLY LANDED NEAR HIM.

I TOLD HIM TO STOP
STUFFING HIS SUPPER
DOWN HIS PANTS.

DINNER WAS NOT SERVED
QUICKLY ENOUGH.

REASONS · WHY · *I'M* · CRYING

- I asked him to stop using his spoon to catapult his peas across the table, one by one, like a medieval fortress siege.

- I politely asked him to stop sitting on his brother's head.

- I wouldn't let him stick a garden hose down his brother's pants.

- He happily invited me to "feel his sleeve." I did. He immediately lost his mind and said, "NOOOOO! NOT WITH YOUR HANDS!!!"

- I secretly suggested we get ice cream by spelling the word to my wife—and was immediately busted by the three-year-old, because I-C-E sounds exactly like *ice cream*.

HE WAS TRYING TO PUT HIS UNDERWEAR ON HIS HEAD. I HELPED.

3

NO SHIRT, NO SHOES, NO TANTRUM

From the earliest of ages, toddlers develop a fashion sense all their own. They have very strong opinions when it comes to their preferred wardrobe—and comfort is king. Why wear jeans when you can wear "soft pants"—or better yet, NOTHING AT ALL! From their shouts of *I can do it myself* while hopelessly lost inside their turtlenecks to their endless battles against shirt tags of all types, clothing your toddler is such a struggle that you find yourself seriously considering moving to a warmer climate.

SHE TOOK OFF HER
SANDAL, THEN
COULDN'T PUT IT
BACK ON.

I WOULDN'T LET
HIM GO OUTSIDE IN
DADDY'S SHOES.

HE DIDN'T LIKE THIS
MONKEY OUTFIT.

SHE DIDN'T WANT TO BE A SAILOR LIKE HER SISTER.

57

HE TOOK OFF HIS SHOES AND SOCKS. HIS FEET ARE NOW COLD.

HE WANTED TO WEAR
SOCKS AND FLIP-FLOPS.

I TOLD HIM HE DIDN'T NEED THAT BAND-AID ANYMORE.

I TOOK OFF HIS
WINTER COAT WHEN
HE GOT HOME.

HE DIDN'T LIKE
ANY OF THE
FORTY-SIX PAIRS
OF SWIMSUITS I
OFFERED HIM.

62

DISPATCHES • FROM • THE • FRONT • LINES

One of my wife's biggest complaints about having boys is that there just aren't as many "cute" clothes for them as there are for girls. But she perseveres, scouring stores in search of outfits that will make our boys look like the most handsome prep-school gentlemen you've ever seen.

Those outfits are pristine, unworn, and hanging in the closet.

And in their place? Pajamas. At all times. We secretly hope that, when our boys grow up and perhaps get married, they'll be wearing beautifully cut suits, dazzlingly shined shoes, and elegant ties. But the smart money is on Buzz Lightyear pajamas with rocket wings.

I RECENTLY TOOK UP KNITTING AS A HOBBY.

WE HAD HIM
TRY ON HIS NEW
SWEATER.

HE WANTS TO
WEAR HIS BROWN
SHOES.

66

HE WANTS HIM TO WEAR
HIS YELLOW SHOES.

HIS TRAIN DERAILED.

68

4

E.T. . . . THE EXASPERATED TODDLER

As newly arrived visitors to our world,
children are seeing everything on our planet
for the first time. Our advanced technologies
confuse and enrage them. Zippers are their
vicious metal-toothed foes. Light switches are
tauntingly placed far above their reach,
and universal remotes are covered with
hieroglyphs that must somehow be decoded
before Elmo will appear. Yes, the world can
be a confusing place for all of us—but especially
so for a two-year-old who thinks Newton's
Third Law has something to do with figs.

THE DIAPER IS GONE.

BUZZ
LIGHTYEAR'S
KNEE IS BENT.

71

THE MODEM
STOPPED FLASHING.

I WOULDN'T LET
HIM ELECTROCUTE
HIMSELF.

THE SLIDE IS NOT SLIPPERY
ENOUGH.

THE DOG WAS IN THE WAY WHILE HE WAS TRYING TO PUSH THE CHAIR.

T-REX'S JAW IS NOT BIG ENOUGH TO BITE THIS LEGO-MAN'S HEAD.

76

THE REMOTE-
CONTROLLED CAR
HE WAS DRIVING
DROVE AWAY.

REASONS · WHY · *I'M* · CRYING

- We saw a dragonfly. My son reacted like he was being attacked by a pterodactyl.

- Why do those we love most try so hard to gouge out our eyes with Matchbox cars?

- Despite my repeated pleadings, he has successfully hidden his water cup from himself again. Does that make him the winner or the loser of this game?

- My three-year-old is super, super helpful . . . as long as the task at hand is opening all his brother's birthday presents—and not sharing them.

- He gave his Slinky Dog toy to his little brother. His brother happily accepted. CUT TO SOUL-CRUSHING REALIZATION THAT HE NOW HAS NO SLINKY DOG TOY.

HER DAD IS STUCK IN THE COMPUTER.

HE PUT HIMSELF
IN TIME OUT FOR
NO REASON

5

IF YOU CAN'T DO THE TIME

Toddlers are forever pushing
their boundaries—and your buttons—
to see just how much they can get away
with. Transitioning from caregiver
to crime stopper is all part of the job.
You make up the rules as you go and you
try your best to enforce them, but the
minute your back is turned . . .

IT WAS TIME TO TAKE A NAP.

82

WE TOLD HIM THE BATHTUB
WAS NOT A BED.

83

WE EXPLAINED THAT SHE HAD TO PUT ON HER SWIMSUIT TO GO INTO THE POOL.

I TOLD HIM THE TOILET
IS NOT A TOY.

HE PITCHED HIS TOYS DOWN THE
STAIRS FOR THE THOUSANDTH
TIME AND I SAID HE HAD TO GET
THEM HIMSELF.

HE THREW HIS DINNER ON THE FLOOR AND NOW HE WANTS TO EAT.

HE WASN'T
ALLOWED TO
FINISH EATING THE
DIAPER CREAM.

88

I WOULDN'T LET HIM DRIVE HIS COZY COUPE DOWN THE BASEMENT STAIRS.

89

I TOLD HIM HE COULDN'T RUN UNTIL THEY SAID "GO!"

90

SHE'S NOT ALLOWED TO
EAT GARBAGE OUT OF THE
GARBAGE CAN.

REASONS · WHY · *I'M* · CRYING

- My two-year-old boy opened the door while I was on the toilet. Then my wife and three-year-old came in and we watched as he opened his birthday presents. This is not how I imagined my life would be.

- An eventful day: my two-year-old took a toy screwdriver from the toolbox, walked behind me, yelled "Get him!" and started shivving me in the neck, like in a prison riot.

- Honest admission: My dinner tonight consisted of 100 percent leftovers from my boys' plates. And beer.

- At the last second, I stopped him from drinking the cup of milk that he had successfully hidden in his toy box for at least two days.

- I suggested that maybe the ketchup was best left on the plate—not spread evenly across the table, the chairs, his face, and his brother.

WE STOPPED HIM FROM EATING THIS ROLL OF TOILET PAPER.

93

I ASKED HIM
FOR A HIGH FIVE.

6

LOST IN TRANSLATION

One of the joys of parenthood is
the passing of wisdom between
the generations, the gentle flow of
conversation between parent and child.
Unfortunately there's no Rosetta
Stone software for "toddlerese," so
miscommunication seems inevitable. . . .

WE TOLD HIM THAT HE LOOKED VERY HANDSOME.

I SAID WE HAD TO
CLEAN THE CAKE
OFF HER.

DISPATCHES · FROM · THE · FRONT · LINES

Recently, I tried to teach my three-year-old a joke while we were driving:

"Why did the chicken cross the road?"

"I didn't see any chickens."

"No, I didn't either, but just SAY there was a chicken who was crossing the road. . . ."

"[Concerned] We would hit him with our car!"

"No, okay, what if there was a chicken who wanted to cross the road and there were no cars coming."

"He would FLY. Can chickens fly, Daddy?"

"Well, no. Hmmm. Maybe, for short distances? I'm actually not sure—"

"LOOK DAD . . . A HORSIE!"

It's a work in progress.

ANOTHER KID WANTED TO
KNOW WHAT TOY HE WAS
HOLDING—AND I TOLD HIM.

I ASKED HIM WHAT HE
WANTED FOR DINNER.

I OFFERED HIM HIS
FAVORITE SMOOTHIE.

I OFFERED HIM THE PHONE SO HE COULD SAY HI TO MOMMY.

I PRETENDED MY HAND WAS A PHONE.

HIS TEACHER SAID "NO" . . . TO
SOMEONE ELSE.

SHE BIT MY FINGER.
I SAID "OUCH."

I REFUSED TO PUT
MY OWN HAIR IN A
PONYTAIL.

7

PULL-UPS AND LET-DOWNS

Kids know exactly how they want
their world to work. They have a precise
course of action—a battle plan they
follow to the letter as their day unfolds.
Tragically, they're utterly unable or
unwilling to explain this game plan
to their parents. Even the smallest of
deviations from their top-secret to-do list
is unacceptable. One wrong move, and
you'll unwittingly unleash some of the
most unexpected, unpredictable,
and unreasonable face-down-on-the-
ground flare-ups you have ever seen.

I GAVE HIM PEANUT BUTTER ON A SPOON INSTEAD OF ON MY FINGER.

I LEFT HER HOME WHILE I WENT TO THE STORE TO BUY CUPCAKES.

I WENT TO THE BATHROOM WITHOUT HER.

110

DADDY DIDN'T
WANT A BATHROOM
AUDIENCE.

WE ASKED HIM IF HE
WAS READY TO GO GET
ICE CREAM.

HE DIDN'T WANT TO HOLD MY HAND WHILE WALKING HOME FROM DAY CARE.

WE SIGNED HIS CAST.

I WOULDN'T RIDE
WITH HER (I AM 6'4";
IT'S NOT PHYSICALLY
POSSIBLE).

WE THREW HIM A
PARTY AND INVITED
ALL OUR FAMILY AND
FRIENDS.

WE TURNED ON HIS
FAVORITE SHOW THE
MINUTE HE ASKED US TO.

117

I WENT TO THE MAILBOX, LOCATED ONE FOOT AWAY FROM THE FRONT DOOR.

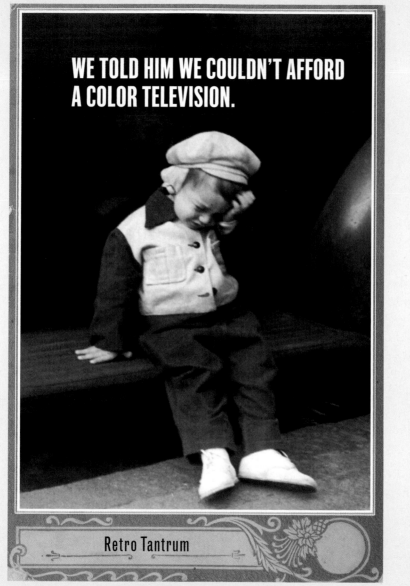

WE TOLD HIM WE COULDN'T AFFORD A COLOR TELEVISION.

Retro Tantrum

PART TWO

HIS AUNT WOULDN'T LET HIM PLAY WITH THIS AX.

8

WE ARE FAMILY

Nothing brings a family together like the introduction of a new baby. The minute that precious bundle of joy arrives home from the hospital, swarms of aunts, uncles, and grandparents arrive—eager to shower these little angels with their love and affection. This doesn't always go as planned.

HE WANTED HIS PICTURE
TAKEN, BUT NOT WITH DADDY.

SHE DIDN'T WANT TO SHARE THE POOL WITH NANA.

125

HIS UNCLE GAVE HIM
A HUG.

DADDY THOUGHT IT
WOULD BE FUN TO TAKE
HIM TO A POOL.

I LET GO OF HIS HAND TO SHOW HIS GRANDMA HOW WELL HE COULD WALK.

WE TOLD HER SHE HAD TO TAKE OFF GRANDMA'S GLASSES SO THAT SHE COULD SEE.

HE COULDN'T CARRY THE BREAKFAST
UP TO DADDY ON FATHER'S DAY.

HIS SKYPE CHAT WITH
GRANDMA AND GRANDPA
FROZE.

SHE DIDN'T
RECOGNIZE DADDY
IN HIS CONTACTS.

GRANDMA WOULDN'T LET HIM
SPILL HIS ICE WATER ALL OVER
THE TABLE (AND HER LAP).

REASONS · WHY · *I'M* · CRYING

- It's 85 degrees and he wanted to wear long-sleeved fleece pj's and a blanket. I said that he might be hot. He vehemently disagreed.

- We arrived at our fifth toddler birthday party in the past two weeks . . . and realized that we had left the gift on the roof of the car. Classic.

- I suggested that maybe we shouldn't put our books, toys, and toothbrushes on top of the toilet. I know! Crazy talk.

- I wouldn't let him take off his diaper and "go commando" while jumping on my bed, directly over my head.

- Sometimes, I stay up wondering what I'm going to step on next in my bare feet. I bet either a grape or a dinosaur. Hopefully not a triceratops.

SHE IS A FLOWER GIRL AT HER COUSIN'S WEDDING.

HE DIDN'T WANT TO
SHARE HIS LEG HOLE.

136

9

SIBLING RIVALRY

Siblings are the best friends we
never asked for. It's no wonder
that the source of the greatest joy
and pain in the lives of toddlers comes
from the people on the planet who
they are genetically closest to.

WE TOLD HER
THAT SHE WAS
GOING TO HAVE A
BABY BROTHER.

HE WOULDN'T SHARE
HIS WATER.

139

I THOUGHT WE COULD TAKE A CUTE "BIG BROTHER–LITTLE BROTHER" PICTURE.

DISPATCHES • FROM • THE • FRONT • LINES

Like most parents, we have extolled the healing virtues of kisses for all manner of injuries over the years, from bumped heads to scraped knees. The other day, I heard my older boy crying. I ran into the bedroom to see his little brother hitting him in the head, and then immediately kissing it to make it "all better" . . . and then hitting him again. After turning my head so they couldn't see me laughing, I tried my best to explain that it didn't work quite like that. . . .

HIS BROTHER DOESN'T
UNDERSTAND WHAT
"PERSONAL SPACE" MEANS.

HER BROTHER SAT
DOWN.

143

HIS SISTER BLOCKED
HIS KICK.

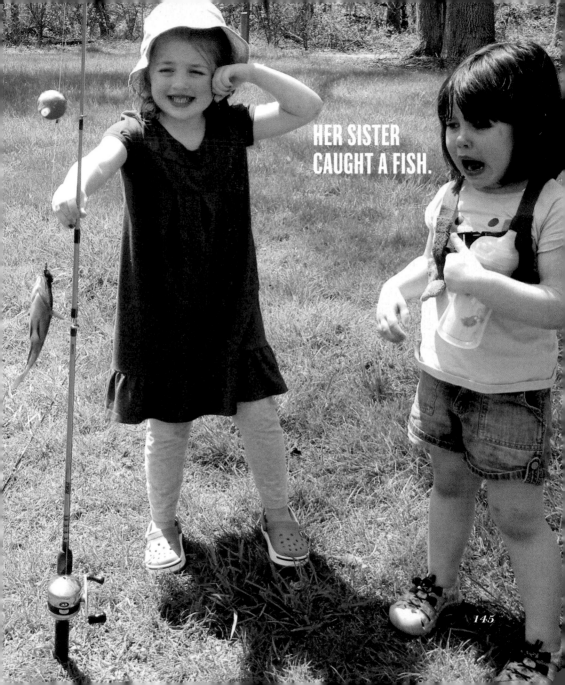

HER SISTER
CAUGHT A FISH.

145

I TOLD THEM THAT I LOVED THEM BOTH EQUALLY.

THEY GOT CAUGHT
BETWEEN THE SPEAKER
AND THE COUCH.

HER SISTER GAVE HER A KISS.

HER BROTHER SAID
SHE COULD GO FIRST.
FOR A SHOT.

149

PART THREE

HE DOESN'T LIKE
THE GRASS.

152

10

CALL OF THE WILD

Almost as important as sleep and good nutrition, time spent outdoors is a critical component of toddler happiness. Like the Lewis and Clark of suburbia, children set forth to explore the world— unfortunately stopping to inspect every pebble, flower, beetle, and ant (and goose dropping) along the way.

WATER GOT ON HIS BATHING SUIT.

SHE HAS TO WEAR A HAT WHILE OUTSIDE.

I WOULDN'T LET HIM PLAY
WITH THE DEAD SQUIRREL
HE FOUND IN THE YARD.

I TOOK THE ROCKS SHE
WAS CHEWING OUT OF
HER MOUTH.

I TOLD HIM THAT HE COULDN'T
GO TO THE BATHROOM ON OUR
NEIGHBOR'S LAWN.

WE LET HIM
PLAY OUTSIDE
IN THE RAIN.

159

THE SAND MADE
HIS FEET SANDY.

THE WIND WASN'T WINDY.

SHE WAS SPLASHED.

HE RAN OUT OF TOYS TO
THROW INTO HIS POOL.

DISPATCHES · FROM · THE · FRONT · LINES

A typical trip to the playground for our energetic explorers can include any one of the following time-honored toddler activities:

1. Crying because I made them go to the playground

2. Crying because no other children are there

3. Crying because too many other children are there

4. Crying because the laws of physics won't allow the swing to go any higher

5. Crying because I won't let them chew old gum found on a bench

6. Crying because I won't let them throw sand

7. Crying because they had sand thrown at them

8. Crying because I won't let them fall from high places

9. Crying because it's time to go home

SHE WANTED TO EAT SAND.
OR, MORE SAND, RATHER.

I PUT HER ON A WOBBLY LOG.

HE COULDN'T WALK THROUGH THE
PLAYGROUND'S SAFETY SCREEN.

THE OFFICERS
LET HIM SIT ON
THIS MOTORCYCLE.

168

11

A key element of safeguarding and shepherding your young charges through the world is to present them with a wide array of age-appropriate and endlessly stimulating educational experiences that they will remember forever. Broadening horizons and leaving an indelible intellectual mark, these unforgettable days form the men and women of tomorrow.

THE AQUARIUM
DOESN'T OPEN FOR
TEN MORE MINUTES.

HE COULDN'T PLAY IN OLD FAITHFUL AT YELLOWSTONE NATIONAL PARK.

OLD FAI

YELL

WE WOULDN'T LET
HIM THROW HIS
DAD'S GLASSES
DOWN INTO THIS
LIGHTHOUSE.

I TOLD HIM THAT WE
WERE GOING TO THE ZOO.

WE TOOK HIM TO A
PETTING ZOO.

174

WE COULDN'T TAKE THE
LIONS HOME WITH US.

DISPATCHES · FROM · THE · FRONT · LINES

We thought for sure that a visit to "Sue," the most complete T-Rex fossil skeleton ever assembled, would be the perfect thing for our dino-loving boys. And it was! Imagine our joy and satisfaction as the boys stared in amazement at this truly larger-than-life creature looming over us.

Then imagine our horror as they attempted to run under the velvet ropes and grab hold of her almost-70-million-year-old legs! As a wise man once said, you can lead a horse to water, but you can't keep a toddler from trying to destroy priceless tyrannosaurus bones.

I WOULDN'T LET HIM EAT THIS UNSWEETENED COCOA POWDER BY THE SPOONFUL.

I SAID I WOULDN'T GIVE
HIM ANY MORE BOOKS.

WE BOUGHT HIM SOME
EDIBLE FINGER PAINTS.

179

THE GOAT GOT A
LITTLE TOO CLOSE.

180.

THE FARM ANIMALS
WERE TOO LOUD.

HE DIDN'T WANT
TO RIDE ON A
TRAIN.

182

HE MET BILL MURRAY.

WE TOOK HER TO SEE SANTA.

12

IT'S MY PARTY

Birthdays, holidays, and
special occasions. It's your time to
make those magical memories that will
last a lifetime. These are the highlights of
the toddler calendar, and all your family
and friends are invited. Welcome to
the Super Bowl of parenting.

WE THOUGHT A PHOTO WITH THE EASTER BUNNY WOULD MAKE HIM EXCITED FOR OUR EGG HUNT.

WE GAVE
HIM HIS OWN
"BUNNY EARS"
FOR EASTER.

187

WE ASKED HIM TO TRY ON
HIS COSTUME, JUST TO
MAKE SURE IT FIT.

SHE DOESN'T
WANT TO BE THE
PINK UNICORN.

189

HE ASKED WHAT
TOYS HE WANTED FOR
CHRISTMAS.

SANTA BOUGHT HIM A
NEW BALANCE BIKE.

191

THERE WERE NO
MORE PRESENTS
TO OPEN.

DISPATCHES · FROM · THE · FRONT · LINES

Holidays are a time when families get together to celebrate togetherness and giving.

Our older boy had a fire truck toy that he loves. Unfortunately, our younger boy soon started to love it as well. The fur began to fly and fights over the fire truck were a daily occurrence, so we decided that a new, identical truck would make the perfect Christmas gift for our two-year-old.

After several weeks of looking, we finally found one for sale, wrapped it up, then waited for the joyful day. Upon opening it, my sons realized that it was indeed identical—except for one single sticker that was torn. Instead of happily playing alongside each other with their identical trucks, the boys then fought over which one would get the one with the torn sticker.

Like I said, holidays are a time when families . . .

WE WOULDN'T LET HIM
TOUCH THE FIRE.

WE GATHERED
AROUND AND YELLED
"HAPPY BIRTHDAY!"

I HAVE NO IDEA WHY
MY SON IS CRYING.

196

ACKNOWLEDGMENTS

I would like to offer my sincerest thanks to the thousands of families who submitted photos for this book and for my website. It's a truly remarkable community that we have established— and I can't wait to see what hilarious photos you'll send me next!

To Charity: Knowing you'll be there for me, for better or worse, is the reason we have so much "for better" and so little "for worse." I promise to someday not spend so much time on my phone.

And of course I would be utterly remiss not to also thank my beautiful crying boys. I know we choose to celebrate some of the silly reasons for your tears, but always remember that the laughter and joy you both bring washes away any sadness, tenfold. The last four and a half years have been an incredible journey, and I cannot wait to relish the adventures, hilarity, and mischief that await us all as a family in the future!

PHOTO CREDITS

Page 14: Kate Halvorson; page 16: Amy; page 17: Jamie; page 18: Benji; page 19: Elissa Kojzarek; page 20: David Barendt and Robin Jump; page 21: The Baker Family; page 22: Rebecca Stachewicz; page 23: Lara Dolly Elliman; page 24: Emily Hannux; page 25: The Sitko Family; page 27: Rebecca Stachewicz; page 28: The Chance Family; page 29: The Gould Family; page 30: The Pembroke Family; page 31: Rachel Lutz; page 32: Alicia Hupageman; page 34: Angie Palmer and Rachel Zabala; page 35: Bethany Beams; page 36: Chloe Wright; page 37: J. Perry; page 38: Sarah R.; page 39: Heidi Ring; page 40: Luke Shinners; page 41: Georgie Kester; page 42: Jessica Metzger and Ingrid; page 43: Ruthann Richardson and Ron Young; page 44: Rebecca S.; page 45: Sidney F.; page 46: Nate Hofer; page 47: The Yee Family; page 48: Melvin, Carey, and Caden Litton; page 49: Kyle and Jamie Anderson; page 50: Finn Jackson; page 52: Stenger Family; page 54: Chloe Wright; page 55: Heather A.; page 56: The Pembroke Family; page 57: The Yaeger Family; page 58: The Pembroke Family; page 59: Beth Mattson; page 60: The Pembroke Family; page 61: Paolo K.; page 62: Myrick Kestenbaum; page 64: The Wallevand Family; page 65: Jesse and Matt Bell (and Andy); page 66: The Pembroke Family; page 67: The Pembroke Family; page 68: The Miller Family; page 70:

Milo; page 71: The Pembroke Family; page 72: Sweet Isla Popageer; page 73: Landon Bixman; page 74: The Pembroke Family; page 75: Leif Christensen and Hunter; page 76: Quentin Jones; page 77: The Natour Family; page 79: Laurie, Joseph, and Adelyn; page 80: Kim Hendricks; page 82: Ben and Kelly Weber; page 83: The Miller Family; page 84: Nicole Aradas; page 85: B. Carothers; page 86: The Pembroke Family; page 87: The Pembroke Family; page 88: The Heskett Family; page 89: Kathy Schwerdt; page 90: The Pembroke Family; page 91: Cheryl Ruyle; page 93: The Rhoads Family; page 94: Jacob Cohen; page 96: Calvin Pence; page 97: Mike, Katie, and Aubrey; page 99: The Frisby Family; page 100: Blake; page 101: The Duzhnikovs of Dubai; page 102: The Watson Family; page 103: Jennifer Avenel; page 104: Anonymous; page 105: Ella Avery and the Capron Family; page 106: Julianne Healey; page 108: Katee and Derrick Sullivan; page 109: Sarah R.; page 110: Anonymous; page 111: The Childs Family; page 112: Jossef Dantas; page 113: Jessica Ainley-Smith; page 114: Kelly Jones; page 115: Grace Stahlman; page 116: Jesse and Matt Bell (and Andy); page 117: Nathan and Rosey Sumrall; page 118: Gayle Kesten; page 119: Sidney Kirschner; page 122: Abbey Moore and Aiden Ferrell; page 124: Kristina Campbell; page 125: Michele Hughes and Madeline Cifuni; page 126: Itay Azriel; page 127: Jillian, James, and Owen Dailey; page 128: The Heskett Family; page 129: cassady jane lorentzen; page 130: Jackson Ramey; page 131: S., S., and Z. White; page 132: The Moskowitz Family; page 133: The Pembroke Family;

page 135: Kate R.; page 136: Cheryl and Martha; page 138: Andrea Bible; page 139: Casper and Abbot; page 140: Megan Barnstable; page 142: The Pembroke Family; page 143: Jennifer Avenel; page 144: Luciano M.; page 145: Heather M.; page 146: The Pembroke Family; page 147: Carlos and Jenny Yepez; page 148: Shannon and Katelyn Ferran; page 149: The Gould Family; page 152: Nicole Aradas; page 154: Zachy; page 155: The Pepe Family; page 156: Amy and Lucas Delmanto; page 157: The Plude Family; page 158: Twist Photography; page 159: Paula and Ethan Brown; page 160: Nathaniel Anderson Patten (by Tina Yee-Patten); page 161: T.J. Hannigan; page 162: Lila Taylor; page 163: Dave Gouveia; page 165: Shilo; page 166: Beatrice Foster; page 167: Wrigley Muldoon; page 168: Lorenzo Yim (Proud of you guys); page 170: Claire; page 171: Molly O'Connor; page 172: Samuel Lamarre and Christine Labrie; page 173: The Hamilton Family; page 174: Jacob S.; page 175: The Hill Family; page 177: The Pembroke Family; page 178: Sarah K. Burkhalter; page 179: The Forr Family; page 180: The Sutton Family; page 181: The Walsh Family; page 182: Andras Szocs and Kathy Kondor; page 183: Laura, Alexander (and Bill); page 184: Jeanne Taylor Photography; page 186: Anonymous; page 187: Jesse and Matt Bell (and Andy); page 188: J.S.K.; page 189: The Oettinger Family; page 190: Andrea K.; page 191: The Thompson Family; page 192: Jennifer Avenel; page 194: Lydia S. and James S.; page 195: Ella Avery and the Capron Family; page 196: The Pembroke Family; pages 202–208: YOU!

"The most viral blog on Tumblr in 2013."
—Yahoo!

"Totally cute (and totally relatable)."
—*Mashable*

One of the Top 8 Favorite Tumblrs by E! Online

A glimpse into the tribulations of parenting that is part documentary, part therapy, and completely hilarious

It all started when busy father Greg Pembroke posted a few pictures online of his three-year-old son midtantrum alongside the reason his son was crying: He had broken his piece of cheese in half. In *Reasons My Kid Is Crying*, Greg presents photos sent from parents around the world, documenting the many, completely logical reasons why small children cry. Among them: "I let him play on the grass," "He ran out of toys to throw into his pool," "The neighbor's dog isn't outside." The result is both an affectionate portrait of the universal, baffling logic of toddlers and a reminder for burned-out parents everywhere that they are not alone.

ReasonsMySonIsCrying.com | ALSO AVAILABLE AS AN EBOOK

"Couldn't be more hilarious."
—*Good Morning America*

"*Reasons My Son Is Crying* makes parents weep . . . with laughter."
—Today.com

New releases, featured titles & more at
ThreeRiversPress.com

THREE RIVERS PRESS

Cover design: Jess Morphew
Cover photographs: *(front)* The Pembroke Family; *(back)* clockwise, starting from top left: Blake; J.S.K.; Kate Halvorson; Melvin, Carey, and Caden Litton; The Chance Family; Andrea K.; Jessica Metzger and Ingrid; The Pembroke Family